COUNTRY PROFILES

ICELAND

BY ALICIA Z. KLEPEIS

BELLWETHER MEDIA • MINNEAPOLIS, MN

Blastoff! Discovery launches a new mission: reading to learn. Filled with facts and features, each book offers you an exciting new world to explore!

BLASTOFF! UNIVERSE

BLASTOFF! Beginners — GRADE K

BLASTOFF! READERS — GRADES 1-3

BLASTOFF! DISCOVERY — GRADE 4

This edition first published in 2021 by Bellwether Media, Inc.

No part of this publication may be reproduced in whole or in part without written permission of the publisher.
For information regarding permission, write to Bellwether Media, Inc., Attention: Permissions Department,
6012 Blue Circle Drive, Minnetonka, MN 55343.

Library of Congress Cataloging-in-Publication Data

Names: Klepeis, Alicia, 1971- author.
Title: Iceland / by Alicia Z. Klepeis.
Description: Minneapolis, MN : Bellwether Media, Inc., 2021. |
    Series: Blastoff! Discovery: Country Profiles | Includes
    bibliographical references and index. | Audience: Ages 7-13 |
    Audience: Grades 4-6 | Summary: "Engaging images accompany
    information about Iceland. The combination of high-interest subject
    matter and narrative text is intended for students in grades 3
    through 8." Provided by publisher.
Identifiers: LCCN 2020001617 (print) | LCCN 2020001618 (ebook)
    | ISBN 9781644872536 (library binding) | ISBN
    9781681037165 (ebook)
Subjects: LCSH: Iceland–Juvenile literature.
Classification: LCC DL305 .K54 2021 (print) | LCC DL305 (ebook)
    | DDC 949.12–dc23
LC record available at https://lccn.loc.gov/2020001617
LC ebook record available at https://lccn.loc.gov/2020001618

Editor: Kieran Downs   Designer: Brittany McIntosh

Printed in the United States of America, North Mankato, MN.

TABLE OF CONTENTS

JÖKULSÁRLÓN GLACIAL LAGOON

On a chilly summer morning, a family arrives at Jökulsárlón. The **lagoon** in front of them has calm blue waters. It is full of floating pieces of ice. Barnacle geese bark and yap as they fly above.

OTHER TOP SITES

BLUE LAGOON

HENGIFOSS WATERFALL

LANDMANNALAUGAR NATURE RESERVE

SNÆFELLSJÖKULL NATIONAL PARK

The family takes a boat tour. Seals play in the waters. In the distance, huge ice chunks crumble from a **glacier**. Splash! Later in the afternoon, they walk to nearby Diamond Beach. The beach gets its name from the glittering ice crystals that decorate the black sand. Welcome to Iceland!

5

LOCATION

DENMARK
STRAIT

GREENLAND
SEA

ICELAND

- - - - REYKJAVÍK
- - - KÓPAVOGUR
- - - HAFNARFJÖRÐUR

ATLANTIC
OCEAN

MORE THAN ONE ISLAND

In addition to the main island, Iceland also owns
many smaller islands. People live on Flatey,
Grímsey, Hrísey, and Heimaey.

NORWEGIAN
SEA

Iceland is an island nation located in northern Europe. This country covers 39,769 square miles (103,000 square kilometers). Reykjavík, the Icelandic capital, is on the west coast.

Waves from the Greenland Sea crash upon the northern shores of Iceland. The Norwegian Sea lies to the east. The waters of the Atlantic Ocean wash against the country's southern and western coasts. The Denmark **Strait** is northwest of Iceland. This body of water separates Iceland and its nearest neighbor, Greenland.

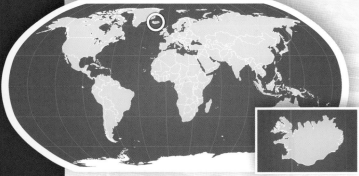

LANDSCAPE AND CLIMATE

Overall, Iceland is a broad, high **plateau**. The center is covered by snow most of the year. Glaciers, including the Vatnajökull glacier, cover much of the plateau. **Volcanoes** such as Holuhraun dot the land. They have created numerous **geysers** and hot springs. The country also has many stunning waterfalls including Gullfoss. **Fjords** cut into Iceland's coastline.

HOLUHRAUN

GULLFOSS

N
W ─┼─ E
S

= VATNAJÖKULL GLACIER

FLIGHT DELAYS

In April 2010, the Icelandic volcano Eyjafjallajökull erupted, sending volcanic ash into the sky. This ash was very dangerous to aircraft. As a result, flights in several European countries were cancelled until air conditions improved.

GULLFOSS

REYKJAVÍK

**Average
seasonal highs
and lows**

JANUARY
HIGH: 37 °F (3 °C)
LOW: 27 °F (-3 °C)

APRIL
HIGH: 43 °F (6 °C)
LOW: 34 °F (1 °C)

JULY
HIGH: 57 °F (14 °C)
LOW: 48 °F (9 °C)

OCTOBER
HIGH: 45 °F (7 °C)
LOW: 36 °F (2 °C)

°F = degrees Fahrenheit
°C = degrees Celsius

Iceland has a **maritime subarctic** climate. Winters tend to be windy and mild. Summers are cool and damp. The northwest gets about 100 snowy days each year. Yet the southeast only gets about 40 days with snow.

WILDLIFE

Many different animals live in Iceland. Trout and salmon swim in the nation's waterways as Arctic terns fly overhead. Arctic foxes feed on birds' eggs and small mammals in the Westfjords. Reindeer graze in the Eastfjords and northeastern highlands. Throughout Iceland, wild mink eat field mice and fish.

Iceland is a paradise for birdwatchers. Lake Mývatn is home to many kinds of ducks such as the gadwall and Barrow's goldeneye. Colorful puffins attract **tourists** from around the globe. The Vestmannaeyjar Islands have a huge puffin colony. Rock ptarmigans and European golden plovers also fly through Icelandic skies.

ATLANTIC PUFFIN

BROWN TROUT

REINDEER

MINK

EUROPEAN GOLDEN PLOVER

NO FROGS OR SNAKES

Iceland does not have any reptiles or amphibians. Its remote location and chilly climate make it so they cannot live there. It is even against the law to have turtles, snakes, or lizards as pets.

ARCTIC
FOX

ARCTIC FOX

Life Span: 3 to 6 years
Red List Status: least concern

Arctic fox range =

LEAST CONCERN	NEAR THREATENED	VULNERABLE	ENDANGERED	CRITICALLY ENDANGERED	EXTINCT IN THE WILD	EXTINCT
▲						

Iceland is a very small country. Only about 350,000 people live in the entire nation. About four out of five Icelanders come from a mix of the **Celtic** and **Norse** people. The rest of Iceland's population have a foreign background. Many people come from Eastern European nations including Poland and Lithuania. A small number are from Asia.

Iceland's official religion is the Evangelical Lutheran Church of Iceland. About two-thirds of Icelanders practice it. Fewer than one out of ten people do not practice any religion. Icelandic is the nation's official language. Students typically also learn English and Danish in school.

FAMOUS FACE

Name: Björk Guðmundsdóttir
Birthday: November 21, 1965
Hometown: Reykjavík, Iceland
Famous for: An award-winning singer and songwriter, as well as an accomplished actress and DJ, she was also named on *TIME* Magazine's 2015 list of 100 most influential people in the world

SPEAK ICELANDIC

ENGLISH	ICELANDIC	HOW TO SAY IT
hello	halló	HA-low
goodbye	bless	bless
please	vinsamlegast	VIN-saam-leh-gast
thank you	takk	tahk
yes	já	yaw
no	nei	nay

REYKJAVÍK

More than nine out of ten Icelanders live in **urban** areas. The nation's biggest city is Reykjavík. It is home to nearly two-thirds of Iceland's entire population. Most people live in apartment buildings. Families typically own at least one car. But people also travel by bus or taxi. In the countryside, people often live in farmhouses.

HAPPY LIVES

In 2019, Iceland was ranked the world's fourth happiest country. Some say this is partly due to a healthy diet and access to beautiful nature.

REYKJAVÍK

SEYÐISFJÖRÐUR

Iceland is a high-tech nation. Nearly all Icelanders use the Internet. Most households are heated with **geothermal** energy. This system uses pipes to bring heat from under the earth's surface into homes and other buildings.

Unlike in many countries, Icelanders do not use many hand gestures when talking. Body language is not an important part of communication. People are friendly but **reserved**, often shaking hands when they meet someone. It is rare to use someone's last name in Iceland. People call each other by their first names, whether a teacher, doctor, or friend.

Icelanders tend to have an upbeat, can-do attitude. A common saying is *Petta reddast*. This roughly translates to "This will all work itself out."

EQUALITY FOR ALL

Iceland is a country that values equality. It was one of the first countries to give women the right to vote. Same-sex marriage became legal in 2010. Iceland was also the first nation to elect a woman president!

Nearly all children in Iceland go to preschool. Students must attend primary school from ages 6 to 16. Most Icelandic students then continue their education at either **vocational** school or junior college. At age 20, students may go on to study at universities. The University of Iceland alone has more than 12,000 students.

Almost three-quarters of Icelanders have **service jobs**. Some work in schools, shops, and offices. Roughly one out of ten people have jobs in tourism. Icelandic workers **manufacture** products such as aluminum and medical supplies. The fishing industry is huge. Frozen fish and other fish products are big moneymakers for Iceland.

TOUR GUIDE

FARMING IN ICELAND

Farmers in Iceland mainly raise cattle and sheep. But they also grow cabbage, potatoes, carrots, and more. Iceland even has a banana farm. It is housed inside a greenhouse!

BLUE LAGOON
HEATED POOL

Soccer and handball are both popular sports in Iceland. People also enjoy playing basketball and golf. The country's national sport is a form of wrestling known as *glíma*. It is common for Icelandic towns to have their own glíma teams. Bodybuilding and power lifting are also very popular throughout Iceland.

SOCCER

Icelanders love spending time outdoors. Skiing, snowmobiling, and snowboarding are winter pastimes. Ice and rock climbing are well-liked, too. Many Icelanders enjoy swimming in naturally heated pools. Chess is a commonly played board game in Iceland. People also meet up with friends at cafés or in their homes.

ICE CLIMBING

PAINT THE NORTHERN LIGHTS

The northern lights occur in the skies above Iceland. Create your own magical landscape using craft supplies!

What You Need:
- white cardstock paper
- watercolor paints
- a few small paintbrushes
- a sponge
- water
- black construction paper
- scissors
- glue

Instructions:

1. Wet your sponge with water and squeeze it slightly so it is not too drippy. Use the sponge to wet the entire surface of your white piece of cardstock.

2. Dip your paintbrush into the paint, then try making different colored layers on the wet cardstock.

3. When the whole piece of cardstock is covered with paint, dab the whole thing again with a wet sponge. Allow the cardstock to dry completely.

4. Cut out mountain shapes from the construction paper. Glue the mountains onto the dried cardstock. Enjoy the view!

FOOD

   Fish, lamb, and dairy products are common in the Icelandic diet. People in Iceland eat a huge variety of fresh and dried fish, including haddock, cod, and salmon. Brave eaters go for *hákarl*, or rotten shark meat. *Hangikjöt* is a popular dish made of smoked lamb. Icelanders **traditionally** eat this meal on Christmas Day. *Skyr* is a yogurt-like dairy product often served with fresh bilberries.

People also eat cucumbers, peppers, and tomatoes regularly. Hot dogs are favorite food, too. Coffee is incredibly popular. Some say that coffee is the country's lifeblood.

HANGIKJÖT

HÁKARL

ICELANDIC COCOA SOUP

Kids of all ages enjoy the treat called Icelandic cocoa soup. Even though it is really a dessert, some Icelanders enjoy it as a main course. Have an adult help you with this recipe.

Ingredients:

3 tablespoons sugar
1/2 teaspoon cinnamon
3 tablespoons unsweetened cocoa powder
2 cups water
3 cups whole milk
1 tablespoon cornstarch (or potato starch)
salt (optional)

Steps:

1. In a saucepan, combine the sugar, cinnamon, and cocoa powder until well blended. Gradually add in the water. Stir until the mixture is smooth.

2. Bring the cocoa-water mixture to a boil on the stovetop. Once it is boiling, turn down to a simmer and cook for 5 minutes.

3. Add in the milk. Bring the mixture to a boil. Again, turn down to a simmer and cook for 2 to 3 minutes.

4. In a little cup, combine the cornstarch with a teaspoon or less of cold water. Stir this cornstarch mixture into the cocoa soup, then take the saucepan off the heat.

5. To enjoy the soup Icelandic-style, add a sprinkle of salt. Ladle into bowls and enjoy!

CELEBRATIONS

New Year's Eve is an exciting start to the year in Iceland. People celebrate with bonfires, parties, and fireworks. In recent years, Ash Wednesday has become like Halloween. Children dress up in costumes and visit offices, shops, and other businesses all day. They sing well-practiced songs in exchange for candies.

Every April, Icelanders celebrate the First Day of Summer. Fun activities include sporting events and parades. In September, Icelanders celebrate *Réttir*, or the sheep roundup. Farmers have friends and family help them round up sheep from their summer grazing in the mountains and valleys. Icelanders celebrate their country throughout the year!

ASH WEDNESDAY

CREAM BUN DAY

Cream Bun Day takes place on the Monday before Lent. On this holiday, Icelanders eat loads of cream puffs, often while chatting with friends and drinking coffee. Bakeries earn a lot of money on this fun holiday.

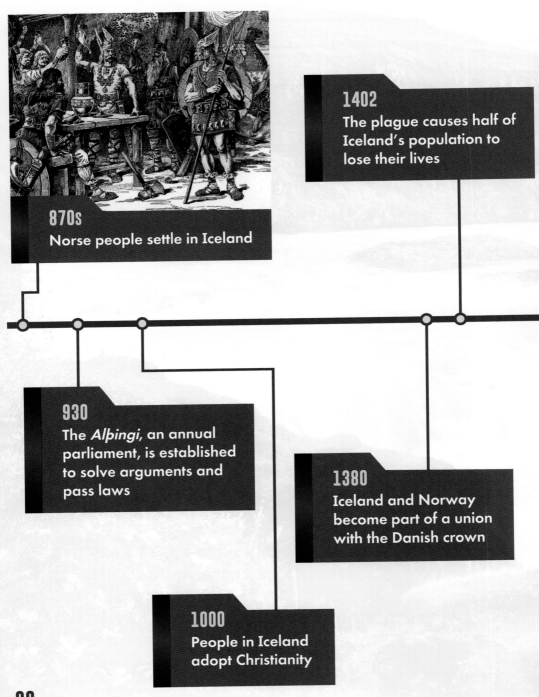

1402
The plague causes half of Iceland's population to lose their lives

870s
Norse people settle in Iceland

930
The *Alþingi*, an annual parliament, is established to solve arguments and pass laws

1380
Iceland and Norway become part of a union with the Danish crown

1000
People in Iceland adopt Christianity

1980
Vigdís Finnbogadóttir becomes the first woman president of Iceland

2018
About 2.3 million foreign tourists visit Iceland

1904
Iceland gains its own government but is still ruled by Denmark

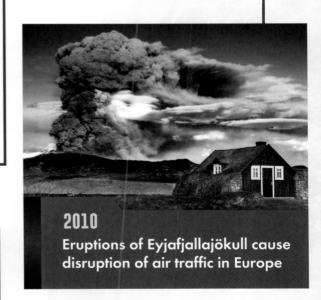

2010
Eruptions of Eyjafjallajökull cause disruption of air traffic in Europe

1944
Iceland becomes an independent nation

Official Name: Republic of Iceland

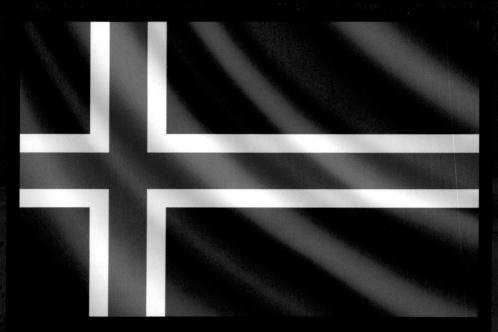

Flag of Iceland: Iceland's flag has a blue background. The blue represents the ocean which surrounds Iceland. On top of the blue is a red cross with a white outline. The red stands for the nation's volcanic fires. The white represents Iceland's ice fields and snow.

Area: 39,769 square miles
(103,000 square kilometers)

Capital City: Reykjavík

Important Cities: Kópavogur, Hafnarfjörður

Population:
350,734 (July 2020)

COUNTRYSIDE
6.1%

WHERE
PEOPLE LIVE

CITY
93.9%

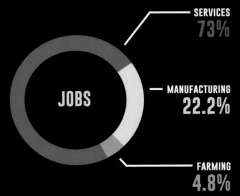

SERVICES
73%

JOBS

MANUFACTURING
22.2%

FARMING
4.8%

Main Exports:

aluminum

machinery

fishing ships

fish and
fish products

medical
products

agricultural
products

National Holiday:
Independence Day (June 17)

Main Language:
Icelandic

Form of Government:
unitary parliamentary republic

Title for Country Leaders:
president (head of state),
prime minister (head of government)

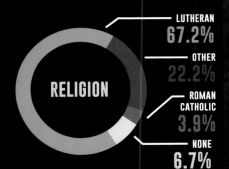

RELIGION

LUTHERAN
67.2%

OTHER
22.2%

ROMAN
CATHOLIC
3.9%

NONE
6.7%

GLOSSARY

Celtic—relating to the Celts; the Celts were early people who spread out from the British Isles and Spain to Asia Minor.

fjords—long, deep inlets of a sea that are lined by mountains

geothermal—relating to heat that is naturally made inside the earth

geysers—hot springs that sometimes send out water and steam

glacier—a massive sheet of ice that covers a large area of land

lagoon—a shallow body of water that connects to a larger body of water

manufacture—to make products, often with machines

maritime subarctic—relating to a climate zone below the Arctic Circle that is affected by the ocean; maritime subarctic climates generally experience cool summers and mild winters.

Norse—related to people who come from northern Europe including areas of present-day Norway, Sweden, and Denmark

plateau—an area of flat, raised land

reserved—cautious in words and actions

service jobs—jobs that perform tasks for people or businesses

strait—a narrow channel connecting two larger bodies of water

tourists—people who travel to visit another place

traditionally—as part of the customs, ideas, or beliefs handed down from one generation to the next

urban—related to cities and city life

vocational—referring to a school that trains students to do specific jobs

volcanoes—holes in the earth; when a volcano erupts, hot ash, gas, or melted rock called lava shoots out.

TO LEARN MORE

AT THE LIBRARY

Burns, Loree Griffin. *Life on Surtsey, Iceland's Upstart Island*. Boston, Mass.: Houghton Mifflin Harcourt, 2017.

Higgins, Nadia. *National Geographic Kids Everything Vikings*. Washington, D.C.: National Geographic, 2015.

Leaf, Christina. *Denmark*. Minneapolis, Minn.: Bellwether Media, 2020.

ON THE WEB

FACTSURFER

Factsurfer.com gives you a safe, fun way to find more information.

1. Go to www.factsurfer.com.

2. Enter "Iceland" into the search box and click 🔍.

3. Select your book cover to see a list of related content.

INDEX